THE BIG BOOK OF
THINGS
THAT GO

A DORLING KINDERSLEY BOOK

Project Editor Caroline Bingham
Art Editor Sara Hill
Senior Editor Sheila Hanly
Additional Design Helen Melville
Production Josie Alabaster

Picture Researcher Joanna Thomas
Photography by Richard Leeney
Additional photography by Peter Downs, Mike Dunning,
Lynton Gardner, Finbar Hawkins, Dave King, Ray Moller,
Tim Ridley, and Alex Wilson
Illustrations by Jonathan Heale

First published in Great Britain in 1994
by Dorling Kindersley Limited,
9 Henrietta Street, London WC2E 8PS

8 10 9 7

A CIP catalogue record for this book is
available from the British Library.

ISBN 0-7513-5200-4

Colour reproduction by Chromagraphics, Singapore
Printed in Spain by Artes Gráficas Toledo, S.A.U.
D.L.TO: 903-1999

THE BIG BOOK OF
THINGS
THAT GO

DORLING KINDERSLEY
LONDON • NEW YORK • STUTTGART

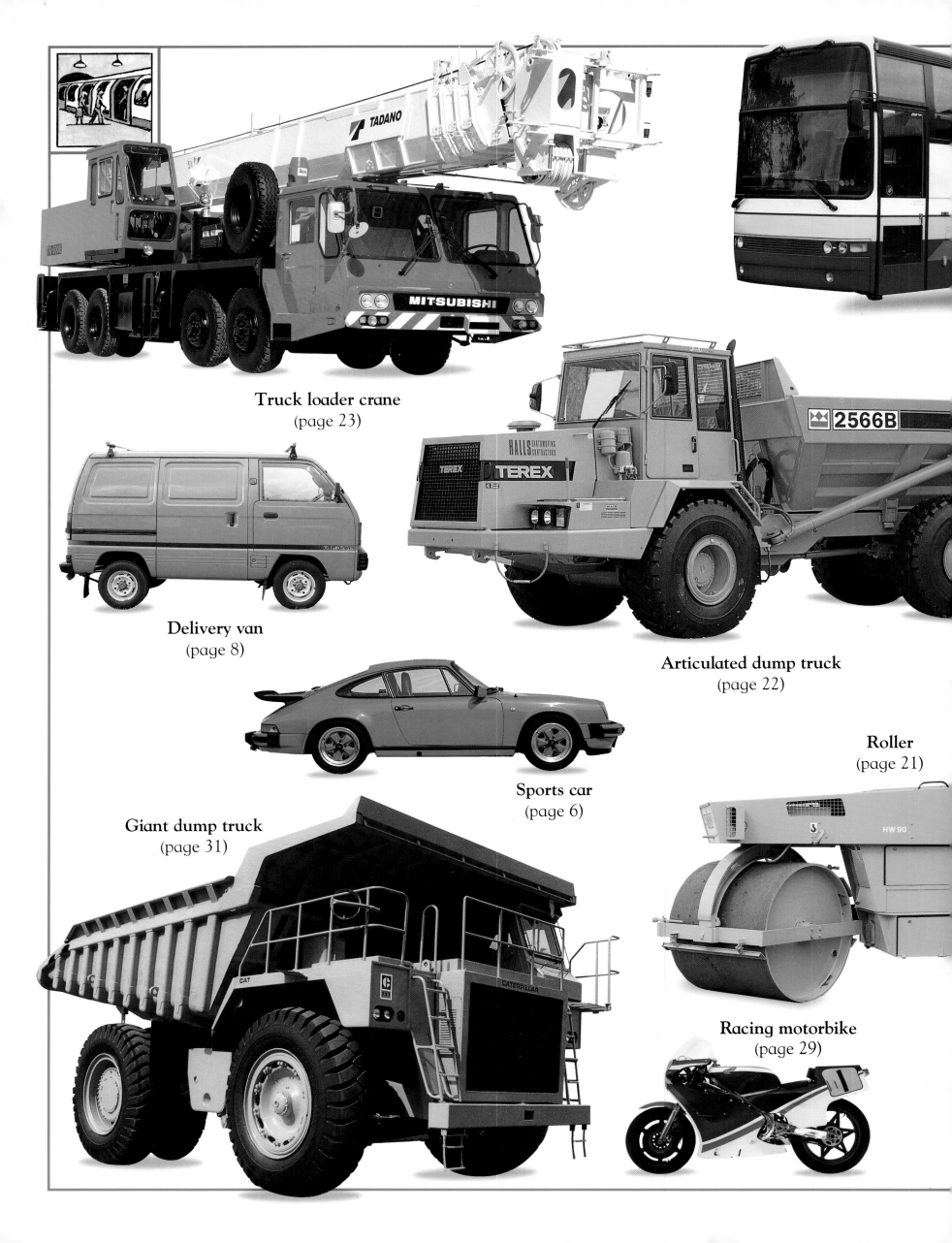

Truck loader crane
(page 23)

Delivery van
(page 8)

Articulated dump truck
(page 22)

Sports car
(page 6)

Roller
(page 21)

Giant dump truck
(page 31)

Racing motorbike
(page 29)

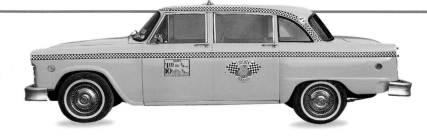

Taxi
(page 9)

Coach
(page 6)

Contents

Hot-air balloon
(page 17)

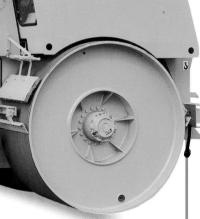

Sailing dinghy
(page 14)

Go-kart
(page 28)

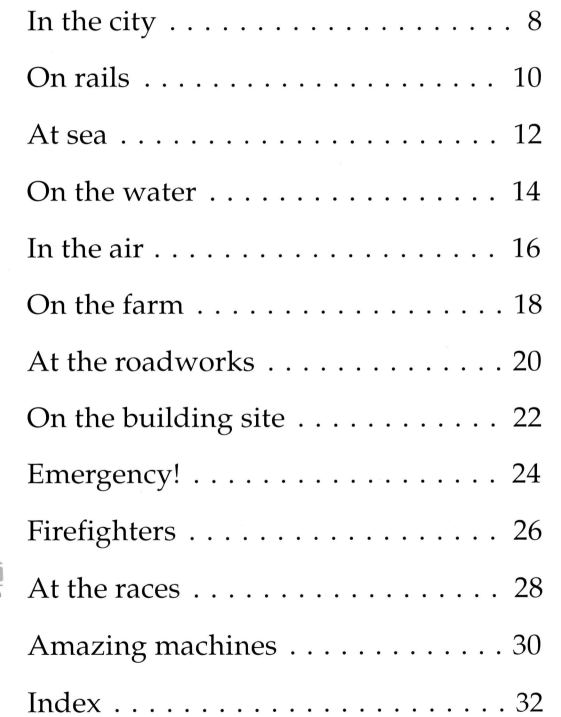

Racing car
(page 28)

On the road

Car transporter

This car transporter is taking new cars from a factory to be sold. How many cars can you count?

Motor caravan

Some people go on holiday in motor caravans. Inside there are beds, a cooker, and even a toilet.

Motorbike

handlebars

Motorbikes have two wheels. The rider steers with the handlebars.

Sports car

A sports car's powerful engine and long, low shape help it to zoom along at top speed.

engine

There is space under the bonnet for luggage.

Coach

Coaches carry people on long journeys. This coach has a special place for bags and rows of comfortable seats.

Bags are stored in these lockers.

Estate car

An estate car has room for five passengers and all their bags. Where do you think the bags would go in this car?

Tanker

Tankers carry liquids in a strong metal tank. This tanker is full of milk that has been collected from a farm.

metal tank

Pick-up truck

A pick-up truck has a flat, open back. It is useful for carrying small loads.

boot

engine

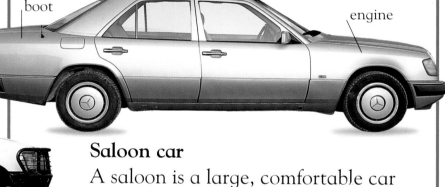

Saloon car

A saloon is a large, comfortable car with four doors. There is space in the boot for luggage.

Transport lorry

Transport lorries carry all sorts of goods. The driver has a special sleeping bunk to use on long journeys.

There is a sleeping bunk in the back of the cab.

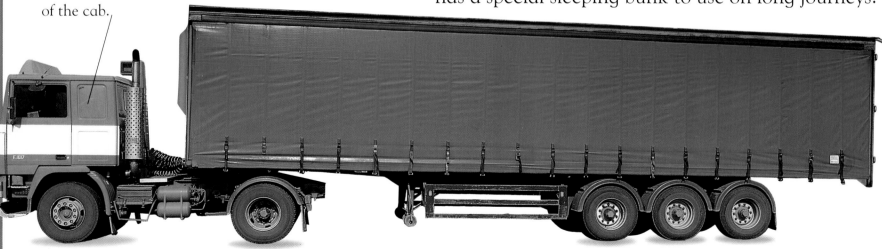

In the city

back
door

Hatchback
This hatchback has five doors. Can you see the fifth door? Hatchbacks are popular cars in cities because they are small and easy to park.

Delivery van
Delivery vans carry goods to shops and to people's homes. A sliding side door makes it easy to load up the back of the van.

Bus
People use buses to go to school and to work. A bus collects its passengers at a bus stop.

side door

Rubbish collection lorry
Rubbish is often collected in lorries like this. Bags of rubbish are crunched up in the back of the lorry.

Bicycle
Riding a bicycle is a fast way of getting around the city. Have you ever ridden a bicycle?

saddle

pedal

rubbish
container

water
tank

hose

Road sweeper

A road sweeper has a big hose to suck up dirt and rubble. It is a bit like an enormous vacuum cleaner, but the road sweeper's hose is wide enough to suck up a brick!

Stretch limousine

A stretch limousine is as long as two hatchbacks put together. Some limousines have a television in the back.

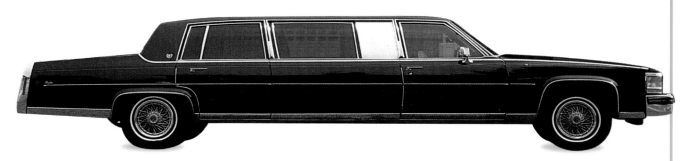

"For hire" light

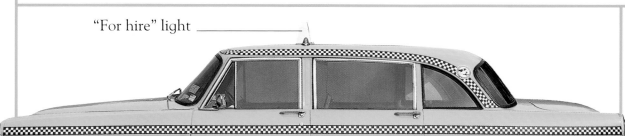

Rickshaw

In some countries, rickshaws are used as taxis to carry people over short distances.

Taxi

People hire taxis to take them wherever they like in a city. This taxi is from New York City in the United States.

Removal van

A removal van carries furniture when people move to a new home. The van is big enough to carry a whole houseful of furniture.

On rails

Steam train

Trains are pulled by engines. A steam engine driver shovels coal into a fire to heat water. The hot water turns into steam, which turns the wheels and makes the engine go.

This wagon, or tender, is full of coal and water.

Diesel locomotive

This engine is very strong. It usually pulls up to 12 carriages along the rails.

engine

Tram

Trams are like buses, but they run on rails along city streets.

Snow plough train

A snow plough train uses large propellers to blow snow off the rails.

Monorail

Monorails run on one rail. They are used to carry people over short distances.

Underground train
An underground train speeds along tunnels built deep under a city's streets.

Rack and pinion train
The rack and pinion train can travel up and down steep hills. It has a toothy wheel that slots into a special rail, like a cog in a machine.

driver's cab

D26

Shunter
A shunter pushes carriages and goods wagons around a railway yard. It needs a powerful engine.

These buffers are used to push carriages.

High speed train
The French high speed train, or TGV, is the fastest passenger train in the world. The train runs on electricity. It picks this up from overhead cables through a pantograph.

pantograph

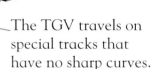

The TGV travels on special tracks that have no sharp curves.

The train is controlled from this cab.

Breakdown train
A breakdown train carries a giant crane. If a carriage comes off the rails, the crane lifts it back into position.

At sea

Catamaran

A catamaran has two hulls. These help it to cut quickly through the waves.

hull

Sub-aqua craft

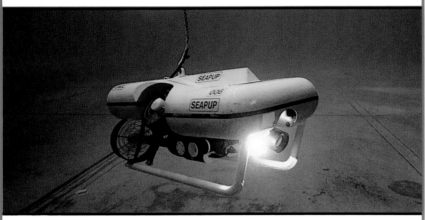

Sub-aqua craft are used to explore the sea bed. They need powerful lamps to light the way.

Outrigger

A wooden float, or outrigger, makes this sailing boat very steady. In some countries, outriggers are used for fishing.

float

Tug

A tug uses steel ropes to pull big ships into port. It can also push a ship into position using its back or stern. This tug has a big tyre on its stern to protect it when it bumps into other boats.

The tug is steered from this room, which is called the bridge.

tyre

Container ship
A container ship carries goods in huge metal crates called containers.

funnel

container

lifeboat

Chinese junk
A junk is a traditional Chinese sailing ship. It has a wide, flat bottom.

Bamboo sticks or battens keep the sail stiff.

Fishing trawler
A fishing trawler catches fish in a large net. The net is pulled along behind the boat.

The net is fed through this frame.

P40

Hovercraft
A hovercraft travels over water on a cushion of air. This hovercraft can carry lots of passengers. It has space for up to 55 cars.

The propellers drive the hovercraft forwards.

Ferry
People use ferries for short journeys across the sea. This ferry has a special deck for cars and lorries.

Passengers can walk around on the top deck.

funnel

These small boats are called lifeboats. They are used to rescue passengers in an emergency.

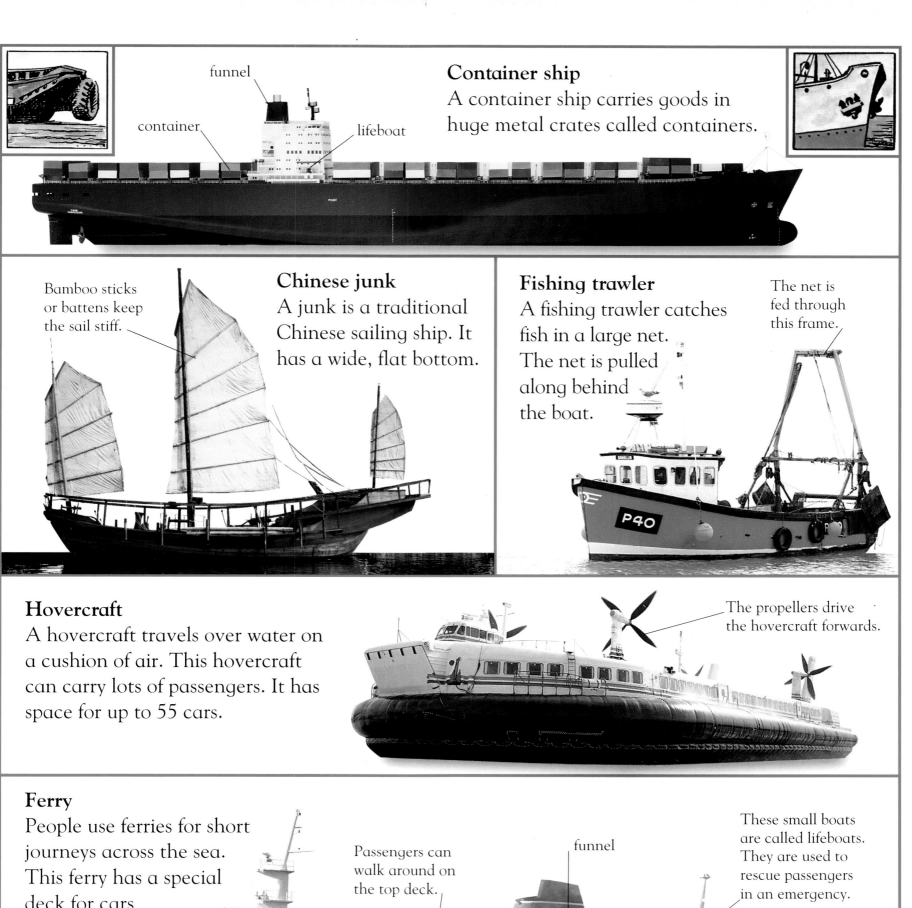

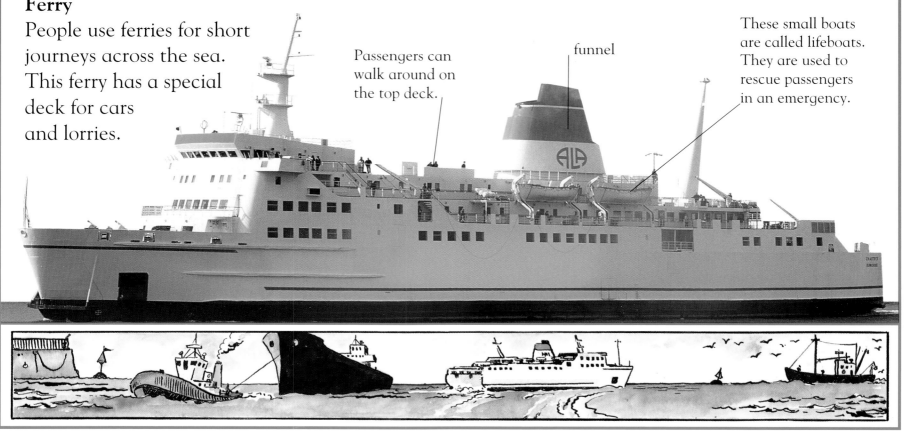

On the water

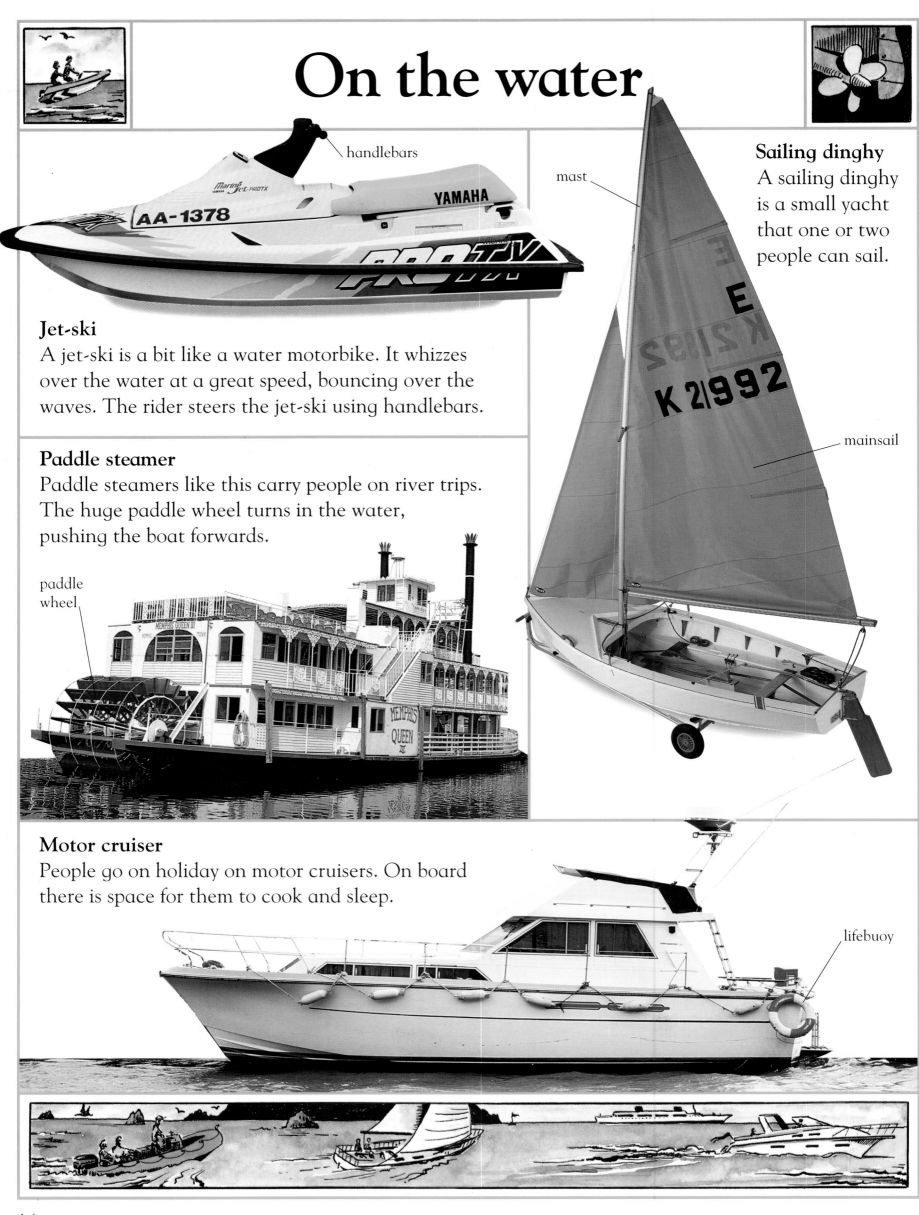

handlebars

Jet-ski

A jet-ski is a bit like a water motorbike. It whizzes over the water at a great speed, bouncing over the waves. The rider steers the jet-ski using handlebars.

Paddle steamer

Paddle steamers like this carry people on river trips. The huge paddle wheel turns in the water, pushing the boat forwards.

paddle wheel

Sailing dinghy

A sailing dinghy is a small yacht that one or two people can sail.

mast

mainsail

Motor cruiser

People go on holiday on motor cruisers. On board there is space for them to cook and sleep.

lifebuoy

Three-masted ship

Big sailing ships like this were once used to carry cargo. They are now used as training ships for young sailors.

square sail

mast

Inflatable

An inflatable is made of strong rubber pumped up with air. It has an engine called an outboard motor to make it skim across the water.

outboard motor

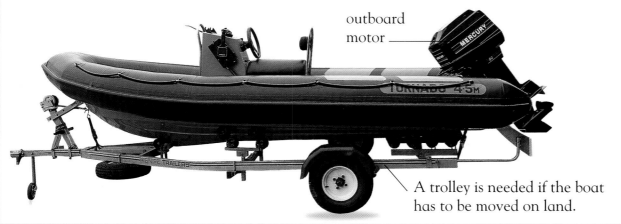

A trolley is needed if the boat has to be moved on land.

Gondola

This gondola carries people on the canals of Venice in Italy. The long oar is used to push the boat through the water.

oar

Ocean liner

An ocean liner is like a floating hotel. It has cabins, shops, swimming pools, and restaurants.

The bedrooms on ships are called cabins.

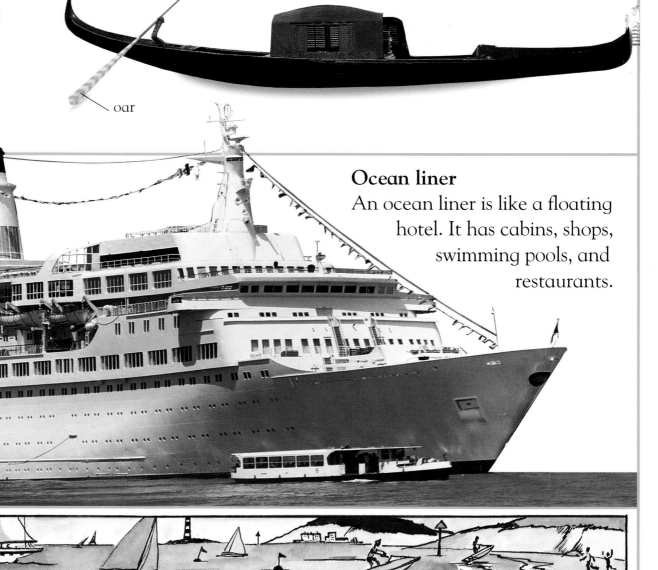

In the air

Light aircraft
Light aircraft are used to carry small groups of people on short journeys.

wing · tail fin · cockpit · propeller · landing wheel

Helicopter
A helicopter has blades instead of wings. They spin round very fast to lift the helicopter straight up into the air.

rotor shaft · rotor blade · tail rotor blade · landing skid

Stunt plane
A stunt plane, or aerobat, can loop the loop and even fly upside down!

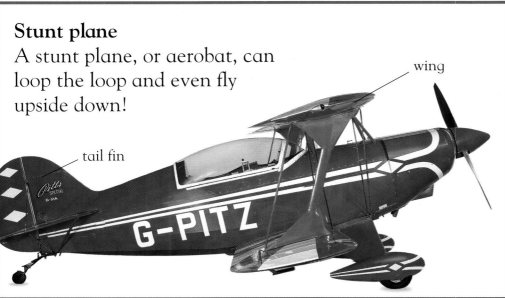

wing · tail fin · G-PITZ

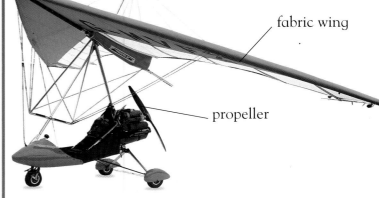

fabric wing · propeller

Microlight
The microlight is a very small plane that pilots fly for fun.

Passenger plane
Passenger planes fly people all around the world, on holidays and on business. Have you ever been in a big aeroplane?

tail fin

Concorde
Concorde flies higher and faster than any other passenger plane.

Concorde's nose drops down when it takes off or lands so that the pilot can see the runway clearly.

Glider
A glider has no engine. It is towed into the sky behind a light aircraft. When the tow cable is released the glider soars through the air.

cockpit

wing

The rudder is used to steer the glider.

Flying boat
A flying boat has a belly shaped like a boat's hull so that it can land on water. Small floats support its wings.

float

G-BMNU

Sea plane
A sea plane has floats instead of wheels so that it can take off and land on water.

Hot-air balloon
This balloon is filled with hot air, which makes it rise up into the sky. Where do you think the passengers ride?

Burners heat the air inside the balloon.

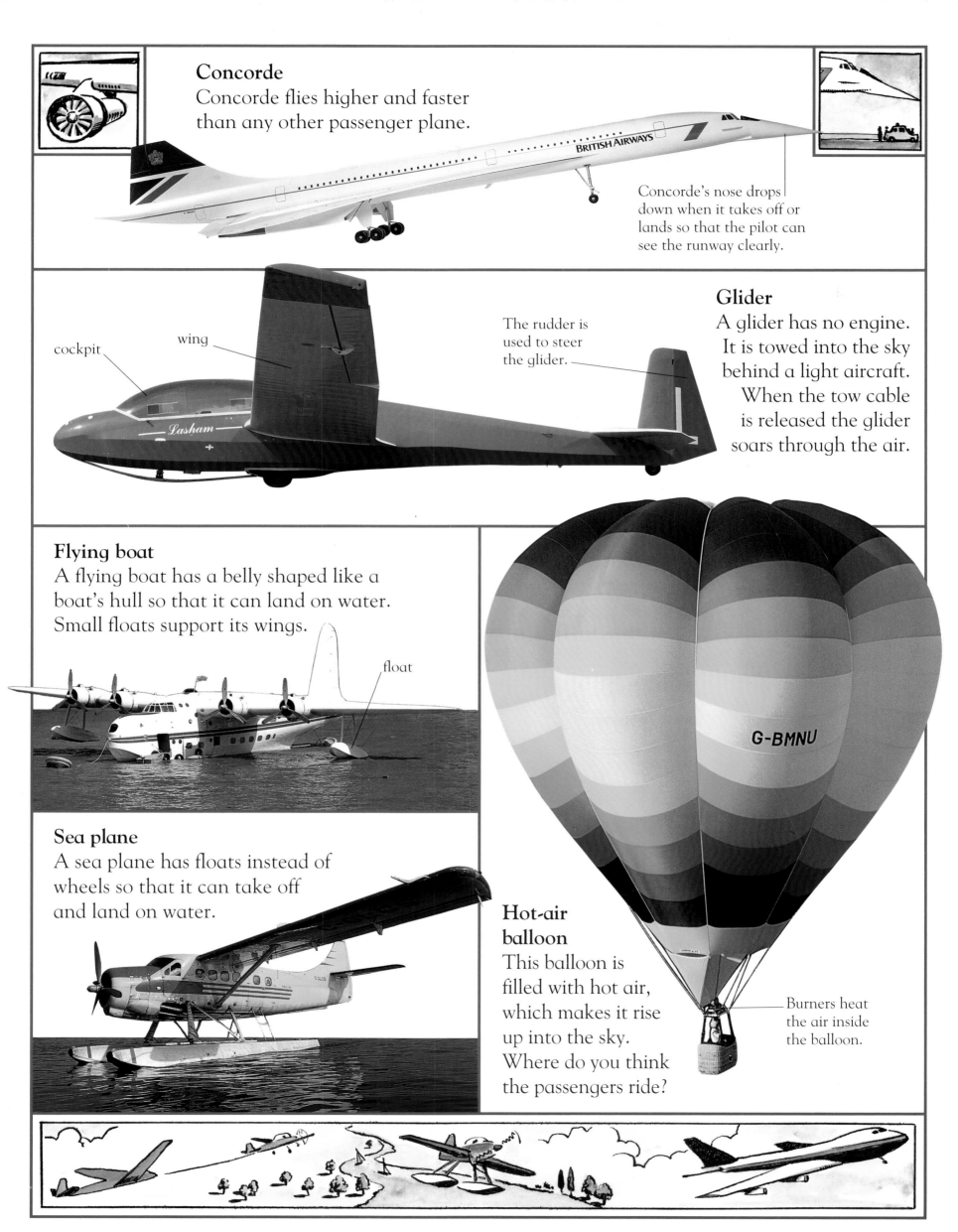

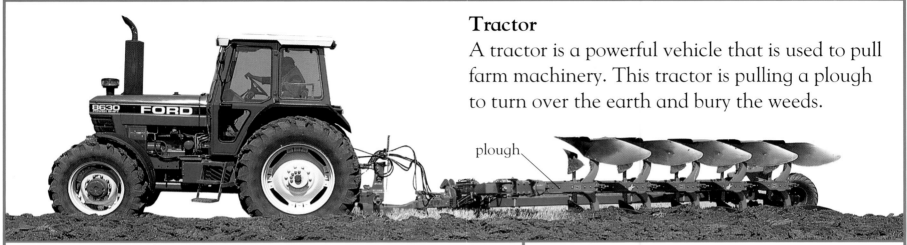

Tractor

A tractor is a powerful vehicle that is used to pull farm machinery. This tractor is pulling a plough to turn over the earth and bury the weeds.

plough

Tractor with furrow press

Ploughed fields are bumpy. The furrow press flattens the bumps and the power harrow smooths the earth.

power harrow

furrow press

Tractor with seed drill

This tractor is planting seeds. The seeds drop into the earth and are covered with soil.

cab

The hopper contains the seeds.

cab

tyre

Multipurpose truck

This tough truck is used for different jobs on a farm. It can carry heavy loads and has deep grooves in its tyres to stop it from getting stuck in the mud.

Forage harvester

A forage harvester collects mown grass and chops it up. The grass is made into a cattle food called silage.

Farm loader

This farm loader is called a Farm Master. It uses its big shovel to carry grain and cattle food around the farm.

cab

The arm or boom supports the shovel.

shovel

All-terrain vehicle

An all-terrain vehicle, or ATV, can travel over any sort of ground. In Australia ATVs are often used for rounding up sheep.

Combine harvester

When grain crops such as wheat, corn, and barley are fully grown they are cut, or harvested, with a combine harvester.

grain tank

Rice harvester

A rice harvester is a cutting machine. It chops down rice plants. These are collected from the field later.

Telescopic handler

Could you lift a bale of hay? It weighs about 20kg. A telescopic handler can lift 64 bales at a time!

Hay bales are lifted on these forks.

At the roadworks

bucket

cab

The legs keep the excavator steady.

Wheeled excavator
This excavator is like a massive shovel on wheels. Its toothy bucket digs deep trenches.

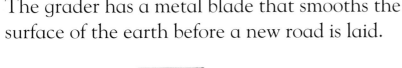

Grader
The grader has a metal blade that smooths the surface of the earth before a new road is laid.

blade

Paver
The paver spreads a layer of warm tarmac over the flattened earth.

The tarmac is tipped into this hopper.

blade

Scraper
A scraper clears a path for a new road by cutting through hills with a sharp blade.

Compactor
The compactor has spiked wheels that squash down the earth.

blade

exhaust pipe

A canopy protects the driver from the sun and rain.

The screed arm lays down the tarmac.

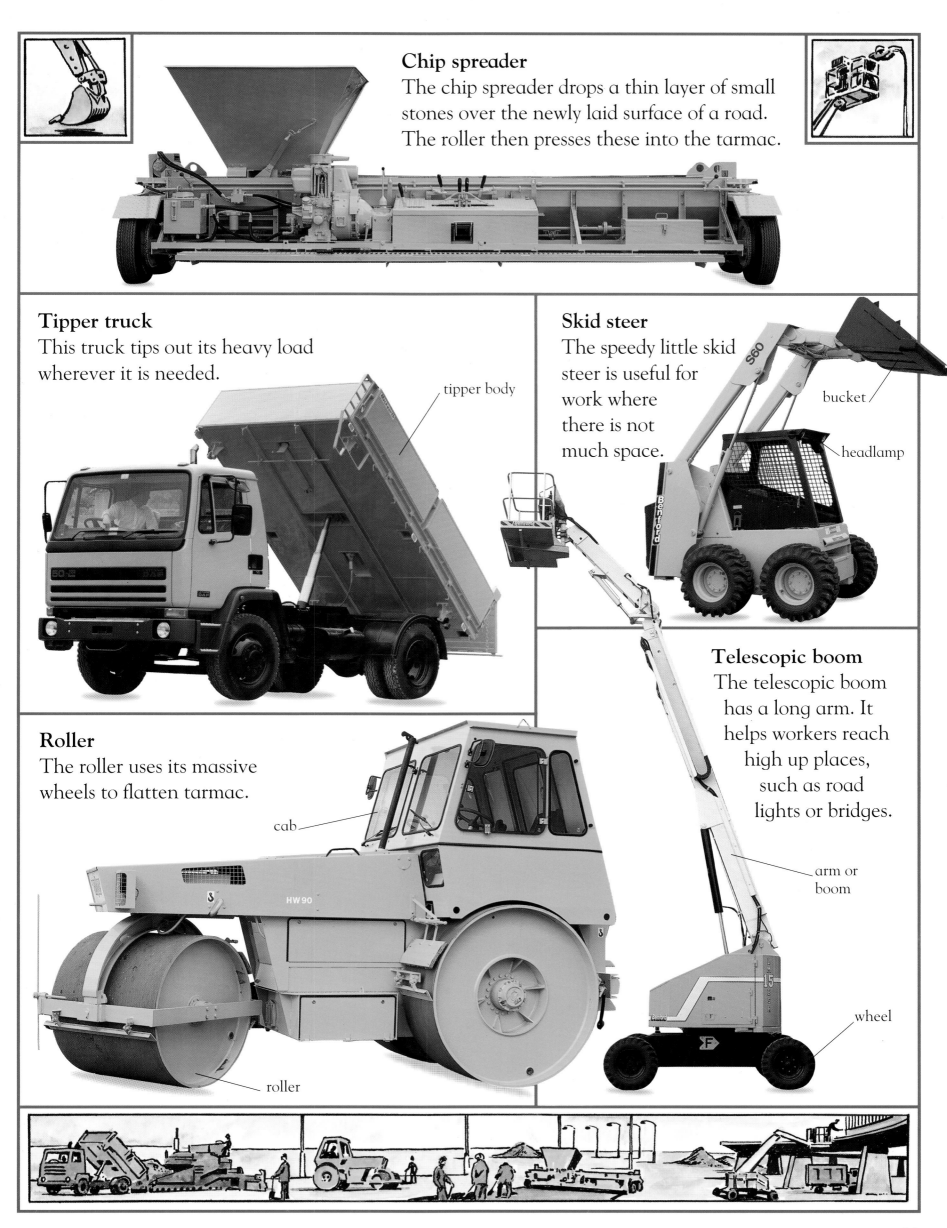

Chip spreader
The chip spreader drops a thin layer of small stones over the newly laid surface of a road. The roller then presses these into the tarmac.

Tipper truck
This truck tips out its heavy load wherever it is needed.

tipper body

Skid steer
The speedy little skid steer is useful for work where there is not much space.

bucket

headlamp

Telescopic boom
The telescopic boom has a long arm. It helps workers reach high up places, such as road lights or bridges.

arm or boom

Roller
The roller uses its massive wheels to flatten tarmac.

cab

roller

wheel

On the building site

Bulldozer

Building sites are full of rubble. This bulldozer uses its strong steel blade to push heavy rubble aside.

exhaust pipe

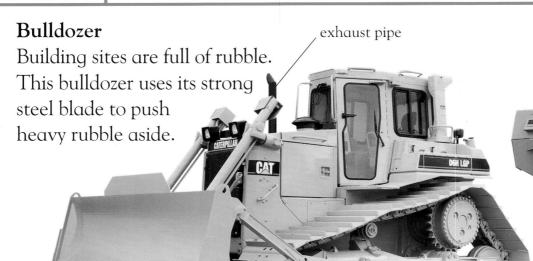

blade

metal crawler tracks

Rubble is carried in this skip.

Dumper

This tough little dumper carries sand, bricks or concrete around the site.

Articulated dump truck

The articulated dump truck carries sand, gravel or stones across the bumpy ground of the building site. The dumper body tips up to empty the load.

An articulated truck bends in the middle.

dumper body

Track excavator

This excavator has a bucket with sharp teeth. These tear into the soil to dig holes.

arm

bucket

Crawler tracks are better than wheels on bumpy ground.

bucket

Wheel loader

The wheel loader's bucket moves up and down, shovelling up earth and stones.

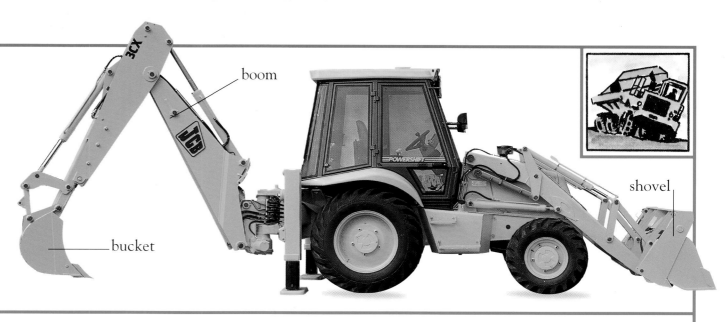

boom

Backhoe loader

A backhoe loader can do two different jobs. Can you work out what it does?

bucket

shovel

Concrete mixer truck

The concrete mixer truck has a big drum that turns round and round to mix concrete. The drum is emptied through a funnel.

Fork-lift truck

A fork-lift truck is used to move heavy stacks of bricks around a building site.

engine

wheel

Skip loader

Skips are used as giant rubbish bins on building sites. Special trucks collect the skips.

crane arm

Truck loader crane

A truck loader crane has an extending crane arm. On a building site, the crane is used to lift heavy steel bars called girders to each new floor of a multi-storey building.

truck cab

Emergency!

Police motorbike

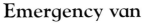

When police have to get around fast, they can weave through traffic on a motorbike.

Emergency van

If a car breaks down, the emergency van might be able to help to get it moving again.

flashing light

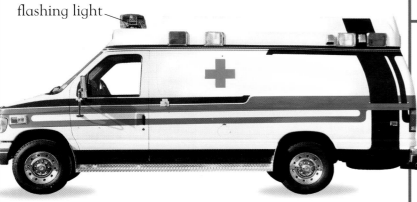

Ambulance

Ambulances rush people to hospital. This ambulance has a flashing light to tell other drivers that the ambulance is in a hurry.

Police boat

In Sydney Harbour in Australia, police use boats to speed across the water to help people in trouble.

Snow plough

The snow plough has a wide steel blade on the front to shovel snow off the road. It clears the way for cars and lorries.

Rescue helicopter
Rescue helicopters are used at sea and over mountains. A winch hoists people up into the helicopter.

Lightship
Lightships are anchored near dangerous rocks and sandbanks where a lighthouse cannot be built. The light warns other boats to keep clear.

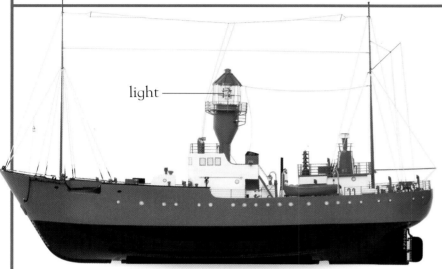

light

Lifeboat
A lifeboat heads out to sea in stormy weather to rescue people in trouble. Radar equipment helps the crew to find a boat in distress very quickly.

Police car
This American police car has a loud siren and flashing lights to warn other cars to let the police car pass.

Tow truck
This truck can tow a broken-down car to the garage. The truck lifts the car with a special frame. The frame has spectacles that slot around a car's front wheels.

spectacles

radar

50-001

50-001

Firefighters

Airport fire engine
An airport fire engine carries huge amounts of water and foam. The water and foam mixture is squirted on to a fire through the monitor.

ladder

monitor

4

JAVELIN

This platform can hold four people.

boom

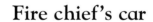

Fire chief's car
This fire car races to the scene of a fire. It gets there before the other fire engines. This gives the chief fire officer time to decide how to put out the fire.

Skylift engine
A skylift engine can hoist a firefighter up to meet the flames of a fire. A water hose runs up the boom, and the firefighter points it at the flames.

Fire rescue truck
This American truck carries special fire-fighting equipment such as saws, hammers, and axes. It gives extra support to other fire engines.

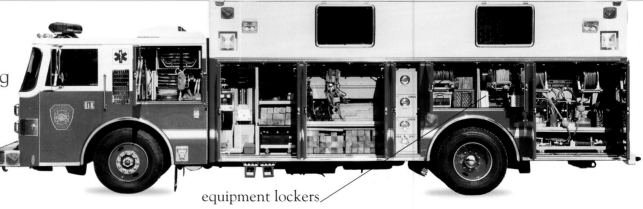

equipment lockers

ladder

hoses

Water tender engine
The water tender engine carries a tank of water. Can you see the hoses, lined up and ready to use?

Rapid intervention vehicle
Rapid intervention vehicles like this are sometimes used at airports. They can reach a fire faster than a big truck.

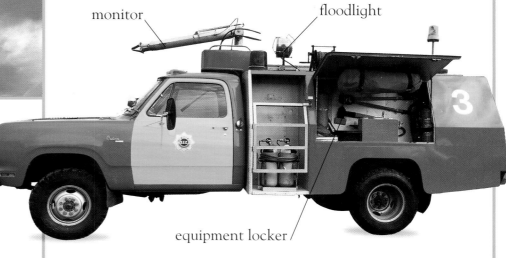

monitor

floodlight

3

equipment locker

Fire fighting aircraft
This aircraft is fighting a forest fire. It has special water tanks which it fills by swooping down across the surface of a lake. The water tanks are emptied over the fire.

Articulated fire truck
This fire truck is articulated, which means that it bends in the middle. This helps the driver to steer over bumpy or muddy ground.

WITTMAN FIELD AIRPORT
WINNEBAGO COUNTY
19

WFA

At the races

Racing car
A racing car hugs the ground as it roars round a race track.

Go-kart
Go-karts are small racing machines. They are driven round special tracks.

engine

Off-road racer
Off-road racing means a bumpy ride for the driver and passenger. The cars often bounce up into the air!

Motocross bike
Motocross bikes race over rocky and muddy ground, and up steep hills.

Powerboat
A powerboat has a long, narrow shape and a powerful engine. This helps it to slice through the water at top speed.

hull

Racing motorbike

This motorbike races at high speed on a racing track. What differences can you see between this motorbike and a motocross bike?

Sidecar racer

A sidecar racer takes two people. They lean from side to side to balance the bike.

Racing yacht

This racing yacht has a big crew. They have to work hard to make the yacht move as fast as it can. The crew pull on ropes called sheets to change the position of the sails. The sails catch the wind and make the yacht speed across the water.

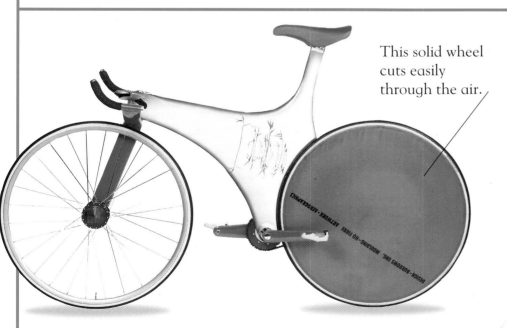

This solid wheel cuts easily through the air.

sail

Racing bicycle

This bicycle is used in races round high speed cycling tracks. It is very light to help it move fast.

Amazing machines

Giant wheel loader
This wheel loader is carrying a massive rock. The rock weighs almost as much as three large elephants!

Harrier
The Harrier jet can rise straight up into the air. It is known as a VTOL jet, which stands for "vertical take-off and landing".

nose cone

wingtip wheel

handlebars for steering

Motorbike
This motorbike was specially built to be the longest in the world.

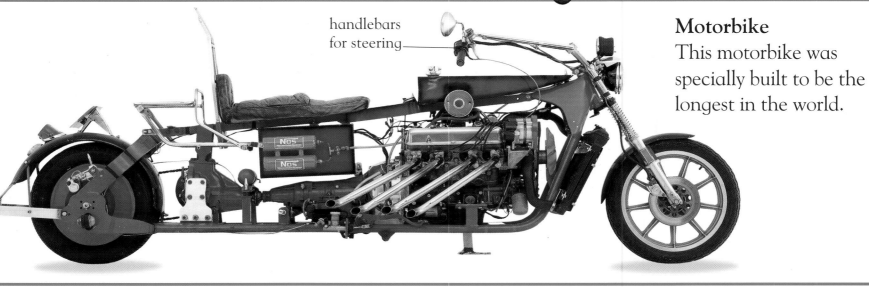

Super stretch limousine
A super stretch limousine is a very long car. It has four windows running down each side.

The windows are tinted so that no one can see inside.

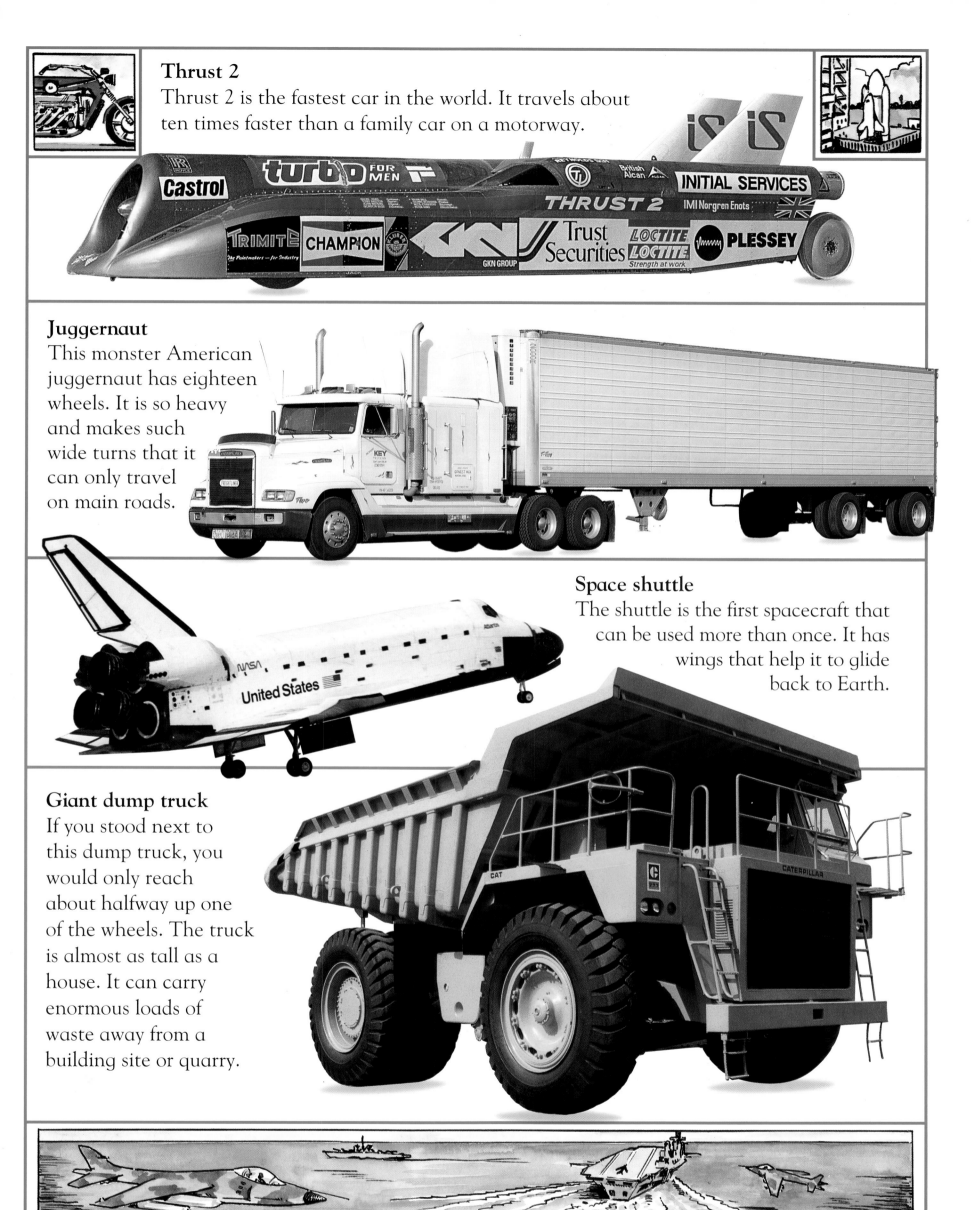

Thrust 2

Thrust 2 is the fastest car in the world. It travels about ten times faster than a family car on a motorway.

Juggernaut

This monster American juggernaut has eighteen wheels. It is so heavy and makes such wide turns that it can only travel on main roads.

Space shuttle

The shuttle is the first spacecraft that can be used more than once. It has wings that help it to glide back to Earth.

Giant dump truck

If you stood next to this dump truck, you would only reach about halfway up one of the wheels. The truck is almost as tall as a house. It can carry enormous loads of waste away from a building site or quarry.

31

Index

Acknowledgments

Dorling Kindersley would like to thank:
Action Vehicles at Shepperton Studios, Middlesex; AirBourne Aviation at Popham Airfield, Nr Basingstoke; Benford Ltd, Warwick; Brands Hatch; Case International; Caterpillar Inc.; G P Edwards; Fairoaks Airport Ltd; FLS Aerospace at London Stansted Airport; Gilmar Motor Engineers; Mark Goss; Griffiths Tucker, Liss, Hampshire; Hoverspeed, Dover; JCB; Johnston Engineering Ltd, Dorking, Surrey; Red Watch at Lambeth Fire Station, London; Lasham Gliding, Alton, Hampshire; John McCluskey; New Holland Ford Ltd; P.J.S. (Agricultural Services) Ltd, Newbury; Harbour Manager's Office at the Port of Dover; S.E.C. Fire Protection Ltd at Shepperton Studios; White Watch at Soho Fire Station, London; Blue and Green Watch at London Stansted Airport Fire Service; Ian Vickerstaff at Terex Equipment Ltd, Motherwell, Scotland.

Picture credits
t=top, b=bottom, c=centre, l=left, r=right, ca=centre above, cb=centre below, cra=centre right above, crb=centre right below, cla=centre left above, clb=centre left below

The Aviation Picture Library/Austin J. Brown 27cl; Balloon Base (Bristol - UK) 5cra, 17br; Pete Biro 28cl; The J. Allan Cash Photolibrary 17clb, 17bl, 24cr; Caterpillar Inc. 20cr, 20cl; Edbro plc, Bolton 21cl and cover; First Waste, Hendon, London 8br; Robert Harding Picture Library 14cl/Ian Griffiths: 10br/Adam Woolfit: 9crb; The Image Bank 10cl and cover, 12cl; London Underground Ltd 11tl; David MacKrill Engineering Group Ltd 23cr; NASA 31clb; National Motor Museum, Beaulieu 31t; Oshkosh Truck Corporation 27b; Quadrant 24b, 25t; Guy Ryecart 28t; Tony Stone Images/Alastair Black: 15t/Michael McQueen: 15b; Tadano-Faun 4tl, 23b; Terex Equipment Ltd 20tr, 30tl; Zefa 10bl, 11tr, 12cr/Bob Croxford: 30cra/Orion Press: 19bl.

Every effort has been made to trace the copyright holders. Dorling Kindersley apologises for any unintentional omissions and would be pleased, in such cases, to add an acknowledgment in future editions.